HAL LEONARD
PITCH PERFEC

A Musician's Guide to

BY ADAM PERLMUTTER

To access audio visit:
www.halleonard.com/mylibrary

Enter Code
4654-4594-3980-1859

ISBN 978-0-634-09778-2

HAL•LEONARD®
CORPORATION
7777 W. BLUEMOUND RD. P.O. BOX 13819 MILWAUKEE, WI 53213

In Australia Contact:
Hal Leonard Australia Pty. Ltd.
4 Lentara Court
Cheltenham, Victoria, 3192 Australia
Email: ausadmin@halleonard.com.au

Visit Hal Leonard Online at
www.halleonard.com

CONTENTS

What Is Perfect Pitch?. 4

What Is Relative Pitch? 6

Other Frequently Asked Questions 7

How to Use This Book 8

Notes and Color. 9

Starting Off on the Right Foot 10

Audiation 11

Session Prep 12

Listening Sessions 12–60

Answer Keys for Sessions 61

Suggestions for Further Reading 80

About the Author 82

WHAT IS PERFECT PITCH?

Perfect pitch—also called absolute pitch—has been a source of endless fascination to musicians and non-musicians alike for hundreds of years. The ability to recognize musical tones with no reference has generally been viewed as a kind of magical power, a gift that only a select few musicians are born with, something that cannot be learned.

But perfect pitch is generally a misunderstood phenomenon. The name itself suggests something black and white, that an individual with the ability can identify any note on any instrument, with 100 percent accuracy at any time. In reality, things are more complex. Perfect pitch encompasses a spectrum of hearing, from being able to identify pitches only on one's own instrument to those on specific instrument groups to those on all instruments; from singing specific pitches with no reference, like a violinist recalling G, D, A, and E (the open strings she's in a habit of tuning) to instantly recalling all 12 tones.

To gain a sense of what perfect pitch means to some musical professionals who have it, I reached out to a couple of former classmates—Jason, a multi-instrumentalist and composer who writes primarily for commercials and soundtracks, and Mary, a music professor/researcher and violinist. We talked about their lives with this type of aural cognition. Here are the conversations we had:

When did you learn you had perfect pitch?

Jason: At a very young age. My mother is a songwriter, and plays piano and some guitar, so there was always music in my house. I remember being five or six years old and having these children's albums, covers of pop songs that were often in different keys than the originals that I heard driving in the car. Even at a young age, this irritated me, though I didn't really yet know why.

I started piano lessons around the same time, and my teacher quickly realized I had perfect pitch. One day she told me to look away from the piano, and I correctly identified the notes that she played.

How did perfect pitch affect you as a young listener?

Jason: I was always fascinated by key changes in songs, particularly really crazy ones, which made my whole world seem to shift—songs like "We Don't Talk Anymore," by Cliff Richard, which has a little pre-chorus that goes into a higher version of the main chorus, then abruptly goes back to the original key. That might seem unremarkable to some listeners, but it was weird to me.

Along those same lines, the Doobie Brothers' "What a Fool Believes" goes through many different key centers. I analyzed it later in life, to understand how it worked from a theoretical standpoint, but as a kid the changes happened so quickly they were like magic tricks. All of this explains why I've always been a big fan of artists like Steely Dan and Stevie Wonder.

What's it like to listen to music having perfect pitch?

Jason: I don't have synesthesia, but I've developed certain associations, both with timbres and pitches. For instance, in my library I've got a synth sound called tap organ, makes me think of a can of grey liver. And I have color associations for certain keys and pitches—associations that I've unconsciously built over the years: to me, D♭ is sort of crystal blue, D is another shade of blue, E♭ is gold, C is red, E is bright yellow, F♯ is kind of purple, and B♭ is green.

Is your sense of pitch absolute?

Jason: Not exactly. Sometimes I'll sing a note without a reference and it'll be slightly sharp or flat. And sometimes I'll get thrown off by something that's in between keys. There's this Police album, *Ghost in the Machine*, that's mastered fast [resulting in the pitch being raised]. When I first heard the album's song "Every Little Thing She Does Is Magic," I had to shut it off, to re-center myself.

Has perfect pitch ever had negative consequences for you?

Jason: Being able to hear the right pitches to play in many situations, it initially hampered my ability to sight-read. But luckily, a lot of my work today involves recording music without notating it, so I don't have to rely extensively on sight-reading skills. However, both my transposing and sight-reading improved with practice and experience over the years.

How does perfect pitch affect your work?

Jason: It's something I use every day in my professional life, though I don't think about it in the moment. If I'm recording a singer who's off in places, I can easily point out the problem areas. If I were to lead an a cappella group, I could give the starting pitch without using a piano. And a colleague and I were editing some music recently and he remarked that perfect pitch allowed me to do the work faster, as I could identify sounds without checking them on the piano.

But wouldn't relative pitch allow you to do that?

Jason: Yes, but that's not how I hear things. I don't hear an F chord as being a perfect forth from a C chord; I just hear it as a vertical slice, an F chord.

When did you discover you had perfect pitch?

Mary: I realized at a very young age; I can't remember not knowing the names of the pitches instantaneously. I must have been five or six, since I started learning an instrument right before I turned five. Maybe I was even younger since we probably had a piano before I ever took my first music lesson.

Can you hear pitches equally well in all contexts?

Mary: I can ID pitches perfectly in many settings/contexts, but I am generally weaker hearing pitch in pop music than in art music or jazz, maybe because of a timbral distinction between acoustic and synthesized sounds.

Can you aurally recall any tone?

Mary: I cannot sing a given pitch perfectly in tune without external reference, but I can definitely sing it within a whole tone of where it should be, or I can match it against the range I know my voice has. I have students with perfect pitch who can grab the right pitch out of the air every time, but I have never been able to do that.

Are there situations where perfect pitch is a hindrance?

Mary: In the classroom, students with perfect pitch might feel bulletproof at certain tasks, but perfect pitch can be their Achilles heel at some tasks, such as singing a given pitch down a minor third. I ask my students, "Do you want to be the musician who can't do that because perfect pitch is in your way, or do you want to be able to do that musical task despite having perfect pitch?"

How has having perfect pitch enhanced your musical life?

Mary: It's made my life easier, but I had to do the work to develop good relative pitch and a solid understanding of harmony, in order to teach ear training and become a much better musician.

MORE THAN YOU KNOW

Many musicians have a more acute sense of pitch than they know. For instance, listen to **Tracks 1–3** of **Audio 1**, an excerpt from the "Minuet in G" from J.S. Bach's *Anna Magdalena Notebook*. If you're ever played the piece, the first and second tracks might sound a little off, but not the third. That's because the first two are played a whole step higher and a half step lower, respectively, than the original piece.

I reached out to another friend from school, Emilio, a pianist since the age of 13 who's long bemoaned his lack of perfect pitch. Out of the blue I emailed and asked if he had a reference pitch. He did indeed have a piano in his office at the symphony hall where he oversees research and curriculum development. "Sing a C," I wrote, "and then test it on the instrument." He wrote back, clearly pleased, "A very low C♯!"

WHAT IS RELATIVE PITCH?

What is relative pitch? How does it relate to perfect pitch? As the name suggests, relative pitch is all about relationships, the distances between notes, both horizontally and vertically. Given a starting note or reference pitch, a musician with strong relative pitch can name any note based on its distance from that pitch. He or she can also identify any interval (the distance between notes), chord type, and so on.

An individual with perfect pitch can name any note without using a reference pitch; can identify the name of each note in a melody, at least one in a moderate tempo, without relying on the distances between the notes; and can identify the individual members of a chord in the same way. Relative and perfect pitch are not mutually exclusive. Although a musician who has perfect pitch can name any note being played, this doesn't mean that he or she has the knowledge or terminology that someone with relative pitch uses to describe the relationships between notes.

To better understand these differences, refer to the following passage of music, heard on **Track 4** of **Audio 1**:

Someone with good relative pitch will identify this as a progression containing major seventh chords, with the roots of the first and second chords spaced an ascending minor third apart; the second and third chords, an ascending perfect fourth; and the third and fourth chords, a descending perfect fifth.

A musician with perfect pitch, on the other hand, will recognize Cmaj7, E♭maj7, A♭maj7, and D♭maj7 chords, even if he or she doesn't know their names. Now, if that individual with relative pitch were told the first chord was an Cmaj7, he or she could fill in the others not necessarily based on the sound of their roots but through his or her knowledge of intervals.

Here's another example:

A musician whose relative pitch is excellent would note that the progression has a common tone in the highest voice, a series of major triads in the three voices underneath, and also that the overall chord qualities are major, major with an added ninth, sixth, and dominant seventh. Someone with perfect pitch would know that the common tone is an F, and would clearly hear the chords F, E♭add9, A♭6, and G7.

Developing relative pitch on its own won't necessarily lead to perfect pitch, but as you'll see in this book's drills, relative pitch can be used judiciously in the process of acquiring perfect pitch. And having a good sense of relative pitch can enhance one's sense of perfect pitch, and vice versa.

OTHER FREQUENTLY ASKED QUESTIONS

How long will it take me to develop perfect pitch?

Within the first week or so you are likely to notice some significant changes. But know that progress rarely comes in equally spaced increments. Some musicians show increased perception from the very beginning, and then level off. Others take a considerably longer time to notice changes before it all comes flooding in. The thread connecting both those extremes is consistent practice, which is the most reliable way to measure your progress.

Once I learn how to do this, will it bother me when I hear instruments that are out of tune, or when I listen to music in different keys?

Instruments being played out of tune probably bother you already, and this has nothing to do with perfect pitch. In some special circumstances, ensemble performers with perfect pitch may be troubled when there is a difference in intonation between the ensemble and the written score. For example, a cellist in a string quartet reads a B♭ in the score and performs the note accurately, but the intonation of the group is slightly flat. Relative to one another the intonation is fine, but compared to an absolute B♭, the cellist may be annoyed by the difference between what is seen versus what is heard. For those who rely solely on their perfect pitch to perform in tune—especially singers—an ensemble performance that drifts in intonation may prove to be challenging. But playing something in F that was originally written in D, for example, will not cause any discomfort.

Do I need to know how to read music?

Not necessarily. There are some notated musical examples, and being able to read them would be helpful, especially for checking the answers, but it's not compulsory.

How does it start? Do I just automatically recognize all the pitches?

No. Interestingly, it's likely you will become increasingly certain that the pitch you're hearing isn't a particular note. In other words, in the beginning you might hear a tone and confidently think something like, "That *can't* be a C♯." This may sound counterintuitive, but in the beginning, that kind of discrimination is just as valuable as positively identifying a pitch.

Will having perfect pitch make me a better musician?

There is no direct correlation between having perfect pitch and one's level of musicianship. So if you're thinking perfect pitch is a cure-all or that it's guaranteed to make you a great improviser, you've been misled. Having said that, there are many benefits to having perfect pitch, and it can certainly enhance your musicianship as a performer and composer.

I find myself extremely frustrated. How do I get to a better place?

It's not unusual to be frustrated in learning tones. Any time it happens, just take a break. Pitch training is not something you can force. And as long as you can approach each exercise as a challenge rather than as a defeat—as well as recognize when it is time to set the book aside—you will be far less likely to become frustrated.

HOW TO USE THIS BOOK

This method is designed to help you develop a sense of perfect pitch. Of course, we can't guarantee that by reading this book you will have absolute pitch. But—unless you're one of the rare individuals afflicted with amusia, the inability to process pitch—if you practice all the exercises in an unhurried and systematic way, your sense of pitch will surely improve. In the process, not only will your overall musicianship benefit, you'll start listening to music on a deeper level and getting more satisfaction from it.

At the heart of this book is a series of 49 ear-training sessions, intended to take seven weeks to complete. Try to stick with one session per day, spending between 10 and 20 minutes. Avoid skipping the work for a few days and then trying to cram several sessions in a day, as the training is best done gradually and consistently.

Many of the sessions include three separate drills; you can do just one and save the others for later, or all three at the same time. Advance to the next session only when you're satisfied with your results on the previous session.

It would also be a good idea to augment your work here with exercises of your own invention. For instance, any time you hear a new song, see if you can identify the key that it's in; work on identifying any of the pitches not produced by instruments that you hear in the background at any given moment.

For all of the work in this book, stick to these three easy guidelines:

1. Station yourself a quiet environment, unplugged from the Internet and free from other distractions. Be relaxed and alert.

2. Never skip an exercise, even if it seems unnecessary for you.

3. Don't strain during these exercises. If it feels like you are struggling through one, take a break and clear your ears, if not for the day, at least for a few hours.

WHAT YOU WILL NEED

Most of the materials for your training are found in this book and on the accompanying audio. Your own instrument would be great to have nearby when doing the exercises, and it would be beneficial to have a piano or keyboard, as well as a chromatic pitch pipe (containing all 12 pitches). The latter will come in handy when you want to test pitches while you're on the go.

Pitch pipes are generally inexpensive, $20 or less, and there are a handful of free or cheap pitch-pipe apps available through Apple. Of course, a real pitch pipe has the benefit of being more immediate—plus, you won't be tempted to check your Twitter feed on it. One more thing: you might also use a small notebook, to help keep track of your progress and record your observations about the ear-training process.

Many musicians rely too much on notes on the printed page, and not enough on what they're actually hearing, so this book uses a minimum of notation. The ability to read music is preferable to working through the sessions, especially for checking the answers found on pages 61–79. A basic knowledge of theory, as well as some relative pitch training, would also be helpful, though not absolutely necessary.

NOTES AND COLORS

The word "color" frequently appears in descriptions of musical tones and keys, as in the note F♯ sounding red or the key of E♭ having a dark-blue tint. Some people with perfect pitch can't help seeing particular colors when they hear music. This condition is called *synaesthesia*, and it isn't limited to pitches and colors. A person with synaesthesia experiences sense-impressions from seemingly unrelated sources—for example, numbers might smell a certain way, or the feel of fabric might trigger a sensation of taste. Statistically, synaesthesia occurs in a very small percentage of people, yet musicians still tend to associate pitches with colors whether they have perfect pitch or not. Why is this the case, and can it be helpful when trying to learn perfect pitch?

In general, it is difficult to communicate our personal, aesthetic impressions of art. Your reaction to a painting by Mark Rothko or to a mobile by Alexander Calder is indefinable and fleeting. It may be quite different than the next person's, since the evaluation of art is largely subjective. We turn to other, more tangible experiences in an attempt to draw comparisons or create metaphors, but at best they are vague approximations. For example, we could try and describe the visual impact of a sculpture in terms of touch, by saying, "You can feel the heaviness of Michelangelo's *Pieta*." This could of course be referring to the sculpture's physical mass or its metaphorical weight.

Music presents further difficulty because it's fundamentally an aural art form; except for printed notation, there is nothing we can look at or touch. Despite the challenges inherent in describing our response to music, it's valuable to do so because it requires us to examine how we perceive and process art. But comparing the experience provided by one sense, then describing in terms of another sense, is often a one-way street.

Using colors to describe keys, chords, and pitches as part of your descriptive language for music may help others better understand what you are trying to convey. However, the reason we refer to it as a one-way street is this: Whereas hearing a tone may generate a color association, it is unlikely that while seeing a color you would make a pitch association. Unless your response was something automatic and akin to synaesthesia, hearing pitches when you see colors is part of a learned response, whether you are conscious of it or not.

A NOTE BY ANY OTHER COLOR

Let's explore the notion of pitch color with an experiment. Listen to **Track 6** of **Audio 1**—the pitch F♯ being played three times. Take some time to consider what color you think might best represent F♯ and fill in the square below using a crayon or a colored pencil.

Now, let a minute or so pass, then take a nice long look at the box and try to imagine the sound of F♯ in your head. Try this for a few minutes.

If you were able to hear the F♯, that's awesome. But, couldn't it simply have been a recollection of hearing the audio, rather than an association between the pitch and the color? Isn't it also likely that, being primed for the task of recalling the F♯, you kept that pitch active in your memory? If the color you chose is really the thing that triggers the pitch in your mind, you should be able to hear it no matter where or when you see the color. Go ahead and try it. Look around the room for something with the same or similar color, relax, and listen for the F♯.

Did you still hear the F♯? If you answer yes, and you feel you really can recall that pitch while looking at the same color elsewhere, then let me ask you this: Was the F♯ you heard in your mind played by a piano? That's because you've got a death grip on the note from the last time you heard it on the audio; your ability to recall it is better described as the playing-back of a memory rather than as "color hearing." You could have looked at the ceiling, down at your foot, the chair, the phone—anything—and have produced the same results; looking at the color had little or nothing to do with it.

It may appear that we're beating a dead horse on the idea of color hearing, but that's not our intent. Instead, we want to be sure you understand that using a color for the purpose of recalling a pitch is no more helpful than using touch, taste, or smell. In other words, crossing the wires between two senses is unlikely to help you learn how to recognize pitches. Even if you feel strongly that certain keys and pitches evoke particular colors in your mind, it's only of use if you can also hear the pitches and keys when you see the colors.

STARTING OFF ON THE RIGHT FOOT

You are about to begin a journey, one that will reveal a great deal about how you perceive and understand your musical environment. Along the way, it's important to be skeptical not only of our claims, but about your results as well. (The preceding exercise with color hearing gave you a taste of what it means to be honest with yourself regarding what you are hearing.) If you can maintain the perspective that you're not learning a new skill, but rather sharpening and integrating an ability that you already possess, you'll be less inclined to feel as if it doesn't work. In fact, there is no "it" to begin with: you're working toward being able to quiet your mind and to allow your senses to do what they do best.

The visual effect of stereographic images is an analogy that comes close to illustrating this idea. These are the kinds of posters that look like random noise, but after you stare at them for a little while and relax your focus, an image appears. Just as those posters require you to look in a new way, learning perfect pitch requires you to listen in a new way.

A curious fact about learning perfect pitch—and ear training in general—is that no matter the method of instruction, everyone acquires facility in a particular and unique manner. That's just another way of saying that simply listing the exercises that did the trick for one musician will not necessarily work for you. However, by presenting the exercises in tandem with the discoveries that precipitated them, you may better identify with what is happening in your own experience, the successes and the failures. The mantra then for this journey is: Always be introspective about how you are able to do the things you can do. If you wait passively for the light bulb to go on, you may be waiting for a long time. Understanding how you learned to connect the dots from A to B will inform your attempt to connect B to C, and so on. The light-bulb moment with perfect pitch isn't when you identify a pitch for the first time. Instead, it's when you understand how you identified the pitch. After that, the rest is just practice.

Now put the book down, reflect on what you've read, and start again tomorrow.

AUDIATION

Imagine that your phone rings—a phone without the benefit of caller ID—and the caller simply says hello to you. Instantly, without thinking, you know who it is. How is it that you can identify the person who is on the phone? Did you memorize the voices of your friends and family? Not in a purposeful way, to be sure. Yet, you are able to put a face and a name with the voice. It is as if the voice is not so much the point, as it is the person—and by extension, places, events, mannerisms, and memories—the voice is attached to. But what does it mean for a voice to be attached to something? For now, here is an exercise for you to try:

First, memorize the following sentence: *I'm hearing voices in my head.*

Once you have it memorized, think of someone whose voice you know well—a friend, a family member, or even a celebrity. Really, take a moment and think of someone. Close your eyes and picture the person you have imagined, and have them say that sentence to you. Keep doing it until you really have heard their voice. Then close your eyes and try it.

The exercise will probably work best after two or three tries, especially if you've visualized what the person looks like and imagine how they would move when they spoke. But pretty soon, in repeating the exercise you'll find that it's as if you're recalling an actual memory instead of making one up—that is how clear it sounds to me. Now try this again with a sentence of your own choosing, writing it down in the box below.

```




```

Now choose two different people whose voices you will try to hear:

1. _____   2. _____

Try this variation of the same idea: Think of a favorite television show or movie, and then narrow it down to a particular character, scene, and line. For example, you might recall the Soup Nazi's antics on *Seinfeld*.

Character: _____   Scene: _____

Line: _____ .

Close your eyes and try thinking of the example a few times.

Generating a sound in your mind, whether it is someone's voice, music, or anything, is called **audiation**. It is the key to developing strong aural skills and learning perfect pitch. What else do you think you could successfully audiate at this moment? By successfully, we mean you can imagine—without a doubt—that particular sound in your mind. Below are three blank spaces. Take a moment and think of three things that, if you closed your eyes and concentrated, would sound crystal clear in your mind—anything from the sound of your alarm clock to your garage door opening. Concentrate intently on this, and write down three things:

1. _____   2. _____   3. _____

Spend some time on this exercise, with the three choices you made. Try this several times during the day and evening, especially right before you retire for the night. Once you can honestly say you have heard those three examples—or even more—pick up this book again and continue.

SESSION PREP

In the previous chapter you were asked to try and audiate a sound that you hear on a regular basis. The next step is to pick those that have a pitch. Try to avoid instances where there is a combination of two or more pitches; for example, some doorbells have multiple pitches as do some standard telephone ringtones. Instead, think of two different items that you encounter on an almost daily basis that provide a pitch, and write them below:

1. _____ 2. _____

The next time you are close to each of the sources, listen to the tone, and hum it. If it's out of your range, just transpose it to a comfortable octave. Keep doing so until you feel comfortable with being able to reproduce the pitch.

This exercise is an excellent way to reinforce your audiation skills. Each time you are about to encounter one of your chosen sources, audiate it first, hum the pitch, and then listen to the source and compare. Work on this for a minimum of two days before going forward. Then, when you're ready, we'll move on to the series of drills that forms the core of this method.

LISTENING SESSIONS

WEEK 1 – SESSION 1

When we learn a new piece of music, our minds become occupied with all the information we're trying to absorb at once—the pitches, rhythms, and layers of elements happening in any given moment, as well as the overall architecture of the composition. Many of us are so busy learning musical literature that we've never taken the time to do something that's incredibly simple but richly rewarding: listen deeply to a single tone.

Whether or not you've done this before, let's take the time now to soak in a single note—one might say the Mother of All Notes—the piano's middle C. Make sure that your environment is free of distractions—that Facebook status update can wait!—close your eyes and play **Track 7** of **Audio 1**.

Listen in a way that is relaxed, but present. It's like this: There's a scenic view you've driven by hundreds of times on the way to work. You've don't really even notice it anymore. Now imagine one day you decided to stop at that place, get out of your car, and spend 15 minutes to take in the scene. You would no doubt encounter so many details you'd never noticed before.

To put it another way, here's what you're doing with the note C: scrutinizing it, listening to it in a way that you've never done before; drinking in the note and letting it sit in your ear.

Now on your own instrument, find a concert C. Trumpeters, this means, of course, to play a D; those on, say, the oboe d'amore should finger an E♭, etc. Play the note repeatedly for at least a few minutes, interspersed with periodic silences. Try to ignore how the note feels in your fingers or in your embouchure, and just focus on its quality of sound.

Listen to nothing for a minute, then try singing the C. Did you nail it? If so, excellent. If not, don't be discouraged—you've only just begun to listen to things in a new way. Let your ears rest until the next session.

WEEK 1 – SESSION 2

Try this: With no external reference, sing the note C. Then, test for accuracy using a pitch pipe, keyboard, or your own instrument. How'd you do? What was the note you actually sang? If it was a C, did the note come naturally, or did you have to labor to hear it in your mind's ear? Write your results and impressions below, or, if you'd like, in a separate journal.

Now let's hone in on another pitch, E♭, the one a minor third above middle C. Just as you did in the previous session with the note C, turn on **Track 8** of **Audio 1**, and really let that E♭ get soaked. It's like marinating a piece of meat or, for you non-carnivores, tofu. If you dip it in a sauce just before cooking it, it won't really take on the flavor. But if you let the protein soak in the sauce overnight, it will be intensely piquant.

To appreciate the flavors of all 12 pitches, we need to give them time to marinate in the ear. Each one has its own distinct taste, of which many of us are unaware, having been conditioned to hear music in terms of relationships. That said, in becoming familiar with the tones it can be useful to hear how they compare to others. So now, let's listen to the E♭ alternated with the C and repeated several times on **Track 9** of **Audio 1**.

What did you hear? How would you compare these two pitches, and can you ascribe a flavor or word to each one? After recording your thoughts below, focus on the concert notes E♭ and C on your own instrument before calling it a day.

WEEK 1 — SESSION 3

Before you delve into this session, see if you can sing an E♭ without assistance. How did it go? Again, if you were unsuccessful, that's okay—pitch recognition can take time to learn. On the other hand, if you were successful, what was your process like? Did you first imagine a C in your mind's ear, or did you go straight to the E♭? Jot down the details here:

_____

_____

_____

Let's revisit the idea of flavors. Your instrument might have many notes—for instance, the piano has a staggering 88 keys—but the good news is that no matter what you play, unless it's a children's diatonic instrument, it has only 12 flavors. The description of each note is highly personal; only you can determine how it feels to you. So, on the piano or other instrument, spend some time with all 12; get inside each note and try to describe the properties that make it unique.

Note Name	Description
C	
C#/D♭	
D	
D#/E♭	
E	
F	
F#/G♭	
G	
G#/A♭	
A	
A#/B♭	
B	

WEEK 1 — SESSION 4

In music, tones—or flavors—are often blended, and to the uninitiated ear, they can be difficult to pull apart. We'll address that problem in this session with some drills involving intervals, the building blocks of music. Intervals are a big part of relative pitch training, because they're all about relationships. But here, we won't be concerned with identifying the distance between the notes or labeling them in any other way. Instead, we'll hear them harmonically (played together) and just work on disentangling the notes and singing them.

First let's work on thirds, both major (remember, encompassing four half-steps) and minor (three half-steps) and their inversions, minor and major sixths (eight and nine half-steps, respectively)—sonorities that have a consonant, or harmonious, sound. All of these intervals will be simple, that is, spanning less than an octave. Listen to **Track 10** of **Audio 1**, and after you hear each pair of intervals, sing the two notes it contains, from lowest note to highest.

On the audio we've allowed a generous amount of space between each example, so that you can pause and hear the tones in your mind's ear before singing. Do this slowly and with concentration. You'll probably know when you've nailed the individual members of each pair of notes. But if you're at all unsure, pause the audio and check for accuracy. Don't worry; at this point, that's not considered cheating.

If you find yourself making mistakes, do a bit of troubleshooting: What is the nature of your errors? Are you singing the highest note before the lowest? Is there one sound in particular that's giving you consistent trouble? Write your findings in the space below, then give your ears a rest for the day.

WEEK 1 – SESSION 5

Before you delve into your next session, try this fun activity: Think of one of your go-to notes for tuning your instrument. For guitarists, this might be an open E; orchestral players might gravitate toward an A 440. Imagine that note, then sing it and check it. Were you accurate? If not, how far off?

Pause for a moment.

Let's now continue aurally parsing intervals. First we'll work on some perfect fourths (spanning five half-steps) and fifths (seven half-steps), which happen to be inversions of one another. (From C to G is a perfect fifth and from G up to C is a perfect fourth.) Playing **Track 11** of **Audio 1**, do the same as you did in the previous session: In your mind, pry apart each pair of intervals, and then sing them, lowest note before highest.

Minor and major seconds, pairs of notes that are a half step and a whole step apart, respectively, can be trickier to pull apart in the ear, as can their inversions, major and minor sevenths (11 and 10 half-steps). But don't let this deter you from trying the drills found on **Track 12** of **Audio 1**, containing simple harmonic seconds and sevenths, both minor and major.

In both of this session's drills, be sure to listen not just for the lower and higher note in each two-note sonority, but for the flavor of each note as well. Don't hesitate to stop the audio, to let any of these sounds marinate in your ear, or to check yourself for accuracy. And even if it feels effortless or even unnecessary to do the drills, run through them anyway.

It might seem as though you're only pulling the notes apart, but something subtler is happening at the same time. If you've followed these sessions diligently and consecutively, then the distinct flavors of the 12 tones are becoming clearer. Whether or not you're aware of it, you're starting to develop important distinctions between each pitch—distinctions that will be more noticeable as you proceed through the sessions.

WEEK 1 — SESSION 6

If you, like so many people, often find yourself tethered to a computer, smart phone, or tablet, then your life is filled with all kinds of digital alert tones. You probably know instantly what each one means, but are you aware of its pitch? To find out, choose one of these sounds, like your phone's ring tone, and see if you can sing, from memory, its primary note or notes before activating the ring tone to confirm. How did that go?

Let's finish our disassembly of harmonic intervals with a pair of more complex drills. The first will include intervals of all types—major and minor seconds, major and minor thirds, perfect fifths and fourths, major and minor sixths, major and minor sevenths, and one new one, the eerie-sounding augmented fourth or diminished fifth (a.k.a tritone, spanning three whole-steps, or six half-steps).

But again these labels are unimportant, at least in the context of working at acquiring perfect pitch. Remember, you're listening for the individual flavors found in each pair of notes. So get to work by listening to **Track 13** on **Audio 1** and singing back those tones.

Once you've spent a little time with all the basic interval types, we'll take things to the next level by introducing intervals that are compound, meaning their notes are greater that an octave apart, as heard on **Track 14** of **Audio 1**. Some of the notes will be out of your range, so you'll probably find yourself hearing the bulk as compound, but singing them as simple, with certain notes transposed to more comfortable octaves.

Jot down some words about your experiences in working with the flavors inside intervals during these last few sessions. If you encountered any trouble spots, be sure to document them below. And if you feel shaky with this session, try repeating it tomorrow.

_____

_____

_____

_____

WEEK 1 – SESSION 7

It's preferable to work on these sessions in the most distraction-free environment. But sometimes when you're scrutinizing pitches, outside sounds can actually be put to good use. Before you dive into this session, take a moment to listen to the sounds around you. Zero in on one, whether it's a car horn or birdsong. Try to identify the pitch by ear, then use an external reference pitch to see how you did.

You've pulled apart two-note sonorities. Let's now work with your ear in hearing the individual flavors in triads, or three-note chords. We'll stick to the basic ones—major, minor, diminished, and augmented, but of course you shouldn't trouble yourself with trying to label them.

As with the harmonic intervals, sing the three notes in each chord from lowest note to highest. If needed, feel free to sing any of the pitches in a different octave than on the sound clip, **Track 15** on **Audio 1**. Try to listen to the individual flavor of each note rather than the chords' overall sonorities.

Remember that it's important to be introspective when working on these sessions. How would you assess your ability to hear the distinct sounds within each triad? Do you see any consistently weak areas? For example, is the middle note the hardest for you to decipher? Why do you think that is? Talk about it in the space below.

WEEK 2 – SESSION 8

Let's revisit our old friend, the note C. Listen in your mind's ear for it and sing it, then check for accuracy. Refer to your notes for Session 2 (page 13) to see what kind of progress you've made. Don't worry if you can't report any improvement—again, this training involves a gradual process, and this is only your second week on the journey.

We'll spend one more session zeroing in on the individual sounds in harmonic sonorities. This first drill, which you can listen to on **Track 16** of **Audio 1**, will have three-note groupings, but will not necessarily be triadic. Some of these sounds might be unfamiliar and harder to identify. This is a good thing, as it will force you to be less influenced by what you already know about pitches in listening for the individual flavors.

Taking things up one more notch, the drills on **Track 17** involve three-note sonorities, bringing compound intervals into the fold. Because of this increase in complexity, each example in the drill will be played twice before a pause for you to sing the notes. Remember to listen deeply throughout and if needed adjust the octave when singing.

How did you do in this session? What, if anything, tripped you up? Were the sounds with notes in close proximity more difficult to pull apart than those based on wider intervals? Before moving on, take your time in troubleshooting, and aim to provide thoughtful questions and answers in the space below.

WEEK 2 — SESSION 9

Begin this session by playing either a C or an E repeatedly, until you feel that you've really got its sound in your head. As before, listen to its character carefully, but in a relaxed manner—after all, this is perfect pitch training, not straining.

Now, after several minutes of working on that, pause for a moment, to refresh your ear. Sing the C or E again, and test yourself. With the note firmly planted in your ear, move on to today's drills, in which you'll be identifying these two pitches, played both melodically and harmonically in different octaves.

Try three groups of 15 (**Audio 1**, **Tracks 18–20**)—or do one now and save the rest for later—and fill in your answers here. For the harmonic examples, label the lowest note first and the highest, separated by commas. (If you hear, for instance, a C and the E directly above, label it C, E.)

Even though you might be using relative pitch, hearing the E as a third away from the C, still focus on the subtle sounds that make these notes unique. Be sure to check your answers with those in notation on page 62, as usual troubleshooting to address any weak areas or recurring problems.

Track 18	Track 19	Track 20
1.	1.	1.
2.	2.	2.
3.	3.	3.
4.	4.	4.
5.	5.	5.
6.	6.	6.
7.	7.	7.
8.	8.	8.
9.	9.	9.
10.	10.	10.
11.	11.	11.
12.	12.	12.
13.	13.	13.
14.	14.	14.
15.	15.	15.

WEEK 2 — SESSION 10

The previous session's exercise is extended to the notes D and F in this session. As before, begin by spending a generous amount of time with each note, focusing on the quality of sound that distinguishes it from the 11 other notes. Get into the D's D-ness and the F's F-ness.

Then, work at identifying your Ds and Fs using **Tracks 21–23** of **Audio 1**. Obviously, with such a limited collection of notes, you have a good chance of getting any example right, but avoid any temptation to plow through these drills with guesswork. Write down what you hear on this page, and check your answers at the back of the book.

When you're satisfied with your progress, give your ears a rest for the day.

Track 21	Track 22	Track 23
1.	1.	1.
2.	2.	2.
3.	3.	3.
4.	4.	4.
5.	5.	5.
6.	6.	6.
7.	7.	7.
8.	8.	8.
9.	9.	9.
10.	10.	10.
11.	11.	11.
12.	12.	12.
13.	13.	13.
14.	14.	14.
15.	15.	15.

WEEK 2 — SESSION 11

We'll now bring the notes G and B into the fold. As before, take a few minutes to really luxuriate in the sound of these flavors. To your ear, what distinguishes one from the other? Is one brighter and the other more subdued? Spend time with the notes to decide for yourself.

Once you've spent some time with the G and the B, play **Tracks 24–26** of **Audio 1**. Things will get a little more involved here—you'll be drilled you on the notes C, D, E, F, G, and B, albeit only melodically. While it's OK if you use relative pitch—for example, if you hear a C, then, in your mind's ear, count the degrees of separation between that note and the next to determine its pitch—at the same time you should be trying to hear the discrete flavor of each note.

How did this drill go? With any luck, your ear is opening up and becoming more attuned to the subtle vibrations that distinguish each of the natural pitches.

Track 24	Track 25	Track 26
1.	1.	1.
2.	2.	2.
3.	3.	3.
4.	4.	4.
5.	5.	5.
6.	6.	6.
7.	7.	7.
8.	8.	8.
9.	9.	9.
10.	10.	10.
11.	11.	11.
12.	12.	12.
13.	13.	13.
14.	14.	14.
15.	15.	15.

WEEK 2 – SESSION 12

Imagine you're at a symphony concert, and all of the musicians are tuning to a single note. Sing the note that you hear in your mind's ear, and test it. If you sang an A, congratulations—you have strong aural recall. Now, on the piano or your own instrument, commune with that A for a few minutes, really getting inside the note. How does it strike you?

The drills on **Tracks 27–29** of **Audio 1** bring the A into the fold for a complete set of natural notes: C, D, E, F, G, A, and B. Again, the goal here is to try to focus on the individual flavors of these seven tones and not so much their relations to each other. So, try to process things horizontally and not vertically.

Having made it through these drills, your journey toward acquiring perfect pitch is well underway. You might also test yourself with a few random pitches. Go to the piano and, without looking, press down on any white key. If you feel at all shaky in doing so, try analyzing the situation: Are you getting certain white notes confused? Spend some time to address the problem before moving forward.

Track 27	Track 28	Track 29
1.	1.	1.
2.	2.	2.
3.	3.	3.
4.	4.	4.
5.	5.	5.
6.	6.	6.
7.	7.	7.
8.	8.	8.
9.	9.	9.
10.	10.	10.
11.	11.	11.
12.	12.	12.
13.	13.	13.
14.	14.	14.
15.	15.	15.

WEEK 2 — SESSION 13

You've worked with all the natural notes; now let's focus on the sharps and flats— C#/Db, D#/Eb, F#/Gb, G#/Ab, A#/Bb. These enharmonic notes have two names of course, but don't be overly concerned with the labels you use in identifying them. Whether you call it C#, Db, Betty, or Al, the flavor remains the same.

Now, blocking out all distractions, take a few moments to soak in the pitches C# and F#. Listen to both notes as if for the first time, even though you have already studied them closely if you've been doing all the work in this book.

The C# and the F# are put to service in the drills found on **Tracks 30–32** of **Audio 1**. Remember to be present when naming the notes, and to listen deeply. You're doing the work not to pass a test but to expand your aural consciousness.

Track 30	Track 31	Track 32
1.	1.	1.
2.	2.	2.
3.	3.	3.
4.	4.	4.
5.	5.	5.
6.	6.	6.
7.	7.	7.
8.	8.	8.
9.	9.	9.
10.	10.	10.
11.	11.	11.
12.	12.	12.
13.	13.	13.
14.	14.	14.
15.	15.	15.

WEEK 2 — SESSION 14

If you've been paying attention, then you might've noticed that there are only three notes that you've not worked with in these pitch-identification drills—D#/E♭, G#/A♭, A#/B♭. You know what to do next: Have an intimate listen to each one, savoring and distinguishing the flavors.

Use **Tracks 33–35** of **Audio 1** to do a series of drills involving all five of the "black" notes—those found in the black keys of the piano. If you ace these drills, nicely done. If not, be your own Monday-morning quarterback. Why do you think you made certain mistakes? Can you see any pattern to them? On the keyboard or your own instrument, spend a little extra time with any of those confounding flavors.

Track 33	Track 34	Track 35
1.	1.	1.
2.	2.	2.
3.	3.	3.
4.	4.	4.
5.	5.	5.
6.	6.	6.
7.	7.	7.
8.	8.	8.
9.	9.	9.
10.	10.	10.
11.	11.	11.
12.	12.	12.
13.	13.	13.
14.	14.	14.
15.	15.	15.

WEEK 3 — SESSION 15

For this session, you'll take a little pop quiz. Don't worry—you're not being graded. The results are for your own edification, to get a sense of where you are with your pitch training. Be analytical with the results. Are certain areas still weak, with some notes harder to distinguish than others? If so, invest in a little time bonding with those not-yet-distinct flavors.

First, listening to **Track 36** of **Audio 1**, write a note name next to each number, choosing from the white-key notes:

1.	2.	3.	4.
5.	6.	7.	8.
9.	10.	11.	12.
13.	14.	15.	16.
17.	18.	19.	20.
21.	22.	23.	24.

Now, play **Track 37** of **Audio 1** and write in the notes you hear; all 12 pitches will be incorporated in this test.

1.	2.	3.	4.
5.	6.	7.	8.
9.	10.	11.	12.
13.	14.	15.	16.
17.	18.	19.	20.
21.	22.	23.	24.

WEEK 3 — SESSION 16

Without help, try singing a C, even if you have previously nailed this activity. Did you find that you retained the note? If not, don't be troubled: Your perfect-pitch acquisition is still a work-in-progress.

In this session's drills we'll take a new approach. Remember, it's important to hit your ear from all sides in conditioning it to be as pitch-sensitive as possible. We'll give you a hint as to the content: In each group of three notes that you will identify on **Tracks 38–40** of **Audio 1**, the first note is a white note and the other two are black notes. While on the surface this might seem like just an exercise in relative pitch, it's more a study reinforcing your perception of the black notes. Think of the Cs as training wheels that will later be removed.

Track 38	Track 39	Track 40
1.	1.	1.
2.	2.	2.
3.	3.	3.
4.	4.	4.
5.	5.	5.
6.	6.	6.
7.	7.	7.
8.	8.	8.
9.	9.	9.
10.	10.	10.
11.	11.	11.
12.	12.	12.

WEEK 3 — SESSION 17

Remember the good old A, the note that the orchestra uses as reference pitch? Try singing it now and testing for accuracy. How did this compare to doing the same exercise with the note C?

The drills here (**Tracks 41–43** of **Audio 1**) are similar to the ones from the previous session. You'll be naming the two black notes that follow each white note, which acts as your security, but there will be greater distances between some of the notes. As always, listen intently for the flavors of the individual tones that are becoming more and more distinct to your ear.

Track 41	Track 42	Track 43
1.	1.	1.
2.	2.	2.
3.	3.	3.
4.	4.	4.
5.	5.	5.
6.	6.	6.
7.	7.	7.
8.	8.	8.
9.	9.	9.
10.	10.	10.
11.	11.	11.
12.	12.	12.

WEEK 3 — SESSION 18

Pick a sharp or flat note—any sharp or flat note. Recall it in your mind and then sing it. Test that note, and make note of what tone you sang. With any luck, your recall is growing stronger and stronger.

Another variation on the white note/black notes idea, the drills found on **Tracks 44–46** of **Audio 1** present a white note followed by three sharp or flat tones, throwing in the occasional complex interval. The tempo of the recordings is a hair slower this time, so that you can really soak in the sonorities as you identify them.

Track 44	Track 45	Track 46
1.	1.	1.
2.	2.	2.
3.	3.	3.
4.	4.	4.
5.	5.	5.
6.	6.	6.
7.	7.	7.
8.	8.	8.
9.	9.	9.
10.	10.	10.

WEEK 3 — SESSION 19

Now we'll revisit all the black notes—C♯, D♯, F♯, G♯, and A♯, or whatever else you'd like to call them. As you did before, take ten minutes or so to play each of these tones on the piano or other instrument, fully absorb them in your ear, recall them in your mind, and sing them.

Without any sort of anchor, like starting each of the previous examples with a white key, you'll be asked to identify pitches, black tones exclusively, melodically and harmonically, on **Tracks 1–3** of **Audio 2**. If you feel the need, you can cheat a little: Pause the audio immediately after the first note you hear, and use an external reference to confirm its name. But as always, really strive for the flavor of each note, and not just the relationships between the tones.

Track 1	Track 2	Track 3
1.	1.	1.
2.	2.	2.
3.	3.	3.
4.	4.	4.
5.	5.	5.
6.	6.	6.
7.	7.	7.
8.	8.	8.
9.	9.	9.
10.	10.	10.
11.	11.	11.
12.	12.	12.
13.	13.	13.
14.	14.	14.
15.	15.	15.

WEEK 3 — SESSION 20

In the last session, if any of the black notes were harder for you to identify than others, take this time to focus on them, listening slowly but deeply as a means of warming up for this session's drills. Can you discover any aural subtleties unique to each note that you hadn't previously noticed?

When you're ready, take a stab at naming the sounds that are played on **Tracks 4–6** of **Audio 2**. Once again, these are all black notes. But this time, some compound intervals will enter the proceedings, making things a little trickier. And as before, labeling the name of a tone—whether, for example F♯ or G♭—is less important than recognizing its flavor.

Track 4	Track 5	Track 6
1.	1.	1.
2.	2.	2.
3.	3.	3.
4.	4.	4.
5.	5.	5.
6.	6.	6.
7.	7.	7.
8.	8.	8.
9.	9.	9.
10.	10.	10.
11.	11.	11.
12.	12.	12.
13.	13.	13.
14.	14.	14.
15.	15.	15.

WEEK 3 — SESSION 21

To begin this session, think about the black notes in your life. If any in particular have been consistently difficult for you to identify, meditate on that tone or tones for a few minutes. Try to get deep inside, to see if you can hear characteristics you had never noticed. Jot down your impressions in your journal.

Once you've spent a while with the session's introductory exercise, try your hand at a new type of drill, found on **Tracks 7–9** of **Audio 2**, in which a C major triad will be followed by a random single note from among all 12 pitches. Again, the C chord acts as a home base, there in case you need a hint based on the relative location of the random notes. In the chart below, fill in only the pitch that follows each C triad.

Track 7	Track 8	Track 9
1.	1.	1.
2.	2.	2.
3.	3.	3.
4.	4.	4.
5.	5.	5.
6.	6.	6.
7.	7.	7.
8.	8.	8.
9.	9.	9.
10.	10.	10.
11.	11.	11.
12.	12.	12.
13.	13.	13.
14.	14.	14.
15.	15.	15.

WEEK 4 — SESSION 22

Do you think you can perfectly recall the note E♭? In preparation to test yourself, review your notes on that pitch's flavors, which you recorded on page 14. Then, listen for the note in your mind and try to sing it. After gauging for accuracy, does the E♭ hold up to your original assessment of its unique sound? If not, why do you think that is?

Give yourself a generous pause before delving into the drills found on **Tracks 10–12** of **Audio 2**. These tests are just like the previous session's tests, but instead of a C triad, they use an E♭ triad as an aural anchor—the sort of anchor that you're on your way to disposing of when it comes to identifying pitches.

Track 10	Track 11	Track 12
1.	1.	1.
2.	2.	2.
3.	3.	3.
4.	4.	4.
5.	5.	5.
6.	6.	6.
7.	7.	7.
8.	8.	8.
9.	9.	9.
10.	10.	10.
11.	11.	11.
12.	12.	12.
13.	13.	13.
14.	14.	14.
15.	15.	15.

WEEK 4 – SESSION 23

Given all the hints that might so far have helped you identify pitches based on their relationships to other notes, you're probably curious as to how your sense of perfect pitch has evolved without reference points. To find out, play **Tracks 13–14** of **Audio 2**, and fill in your answers below. Then, compare your scores with those you earned in the previous two tests, on pages 32 and 33, respectively. First, look for the positive developments you've made and give yourself a pat on the back for this excellent work. Then, look for any lingering trouble areas and address these by refreshing yourself with the pitches or flavors in question.

Listening to **Track 13**, write a white-key note name in each box:

1.	2.	3.	4.
5.	6.	7.	8.
9.	10.	11.	12.
13.	14.	15.	16.
17.	18.	19.	20.
21.	22.	23.	24.

Play **Track 14** and write in the notes you hear; all 12 pitches are represented on the audio.

1.	2.	3.	4.
5.	6.	7.	8.
9.	10.	11.	12.
13.	14.	15.	16.
17.	18.	19.	20.
21.	22.	23.	24.

WEEK 4 – SESSION 24

Are you intimately familiar with any songs in the key of D major or D minor? Or, are you a string player of an instrument that incorporates an open D string? Try conjuring up one of these sources to hear the note D in your mind, then sing it. How did you do? Spend a little time letting the D marinate in your ear before moving on to this session's drills.

On **Tracks 15–17** of **Audio 2**, we'll work with a more limited selection of pitches than in the previous several drills. There won't be a home base, like the E♭ chord in Session 22, but the pitches will be limited to the white notes C, D, E, F, G, A, and B. Each item of the test will incorporate three notes, played melodically, both ascending and descending, or harmonically, with simple intervals. As before, remember to name the notes from lowest note to highest, separated by commas.

Track 15	Track 16	Track 17
1.	1.	1.
2.	2.	2.
3.	3.	3.
4.	4.	4.
5.	5.	5.
6.	6.	6.
7.	7.	7.
8.	8.	8.
9.	9.	9.
10.	10.	10.
11.	11.	11.
12.	12.	12.

WEEK 4 – SESSION 25

Pick a white note—any besides C and D—and subject it to the test: Hear it, sing it, and test it for accuracy. Listen in an undistracted way, and spend as much time as you need with the note until it feels firmly planted in your mind's ear.

The drills you'll do today, found on **Tracks 18–20** of **Audio 2**, will include all the white notes, played both melodically and harmonically, three notes at a time. But this time, compound intervals will be used for some of the examples, which will of course stretch your ears a bit.

Track 18	Track 19	Track 20
1.	1.	1.
2.	2.	2.
3.	3.	3.
4.	4.	4.
5.	5.	5.
6.	6.	6.
7.	7.	7.
8.	8.	8.
9.	9.	9.
10.	10.	10.
11.	11.	11.
12.	12.	12.

WEEK 4 — SESSION 26

Warm up for this session by selecting another white note, seeing if you can recall it without assistance, and spending time letting it marinate in your ear—even if you feel you already know the flavor very well.

Once you're ready, the drills on **Tracks 21–23** of **Audio 2** incorporate all seven white tones, again played melodically and harmonically (with simple intervals), but this time you'll be asked to identify four notes at time. The key here is to really replay each example in your mind before you identify anything, for a better chance at parsing each individual flavor.

Track 21	Track 22	Track 23
1.	1.	1.
2.	2.	2.
3.	3.	3.
4.	4.	4.
5.	5.	5.
6.	6.	6.
7.	7.	7.
8.	8.	8.
9.	9.	9.
10.	10.	10.

WEEK 4 — SESSION 27

Let's focus on the white notes for one more drill. You won't be surprised to find that your first exercise for today is to select yet another white note and see if you can recall it. Then, block out any thoughts or distractions and simply listen, as intently as possible, to the tone for as long as you'd like.

All the white notes appear in the drills on **Tracks 24–26** of **Audio 2**. These exercises are much like the last ones, except that some of the notes are spread across more than one octave. After you've filled in the answers below and checked your work, take a moment to reflect on where you are with your perfect pitch training, and if there are any problems for you to troubleshoot.

Track 24	Track 25	Track 26
1.	1.	1.
2.	2.	2.
3.	3.	3.
4.	4.	4.
5.	5.	5.
6.	6.	6.
7.	7.	7.
8.	8.	8.
9.	9.	9.
10.	10.	10.

WEEK 4 — SESSION 28

Let's bring the black notes back into the fold. Begin by communing with the pitch F♯. Can you hear and sing it without using a reference pitch? Does the note hold up to your original description of it, or are you now hearing additional subtleties of sound.

The drills on **Tracks 27–29** of **Audio 2** follow an easy pattern: pairs of white and black notes. Each track contains 15 pairs; write the pitch names side-by-side, separated by a comma. This time, the tempos of the drills will be a little faster. If you get overwhelmed, feel free to pause the track for a moment to get your bearings straight. It might be tempting to plow through the drills, but sometimes it's best to slow down, to really make sure you're hearing all the flavors.

Track 27	Track 28	Track 29
1.	1.	1.
2.	2.	2.
3.	3.	3.
4.	4.	4.
5.	5.	5.
6.	6.	6.
7.	7.	7.
8.	8.	8.
9.	9.	9.
10.	10.	10.
11.	11.	11.
12.	12.	12.
13.	13.	13.
14.	14.	14.
15.	15.	15.

WEEK 5 – SESSION 29

Now sit again with the note D♯. Try to imagine how it sounds before singing it and confirming the pitch on your instrument or other source of reference. Again, really listen to the note, as if for the first time. Then compare its flavor to that of the other black notes. How does the D♯ stack up to, say, the F♯?

Today's drill, which you can hear on **Tracks 30–32** of **Audio 2**, turns the previous session's exercises on their head. The pattern is this: black note, white note; black note, white note; etc. What's happening with these drills is that the sense of a home base, like a C chord, is being broken down. As you move further along your journey toward perfect pitch, if all is going well, then you have less of a need to lean on such things in identifying pitches.

Track 30	Track 31	Track 32
1.	1.	1.
2.	2.	2.
3.	3.	3.
4.	4.	4.
5.	5.	5.
6.	6.	6.
7.	7.	7.
8.	8.	8.
9.	9.	9.
10.	10.	10.
11.	11.	11.
12.	12.	12.
13.	13.	13.
14.	14.	14.
15.	15.	15.

WEEK 5 – SESSION 30

To begin today's work, focus for a few minutes on the note B♭. Whether or not you can recall it and sing it, try analyzing its flavor. What distinguishes the note from its black-key neighbors? Does the pitch call to mind any songs in the key of B♭?

Played on **Tracks 33–35** of **Audio 2**, the latest drill continues along the same lines as the last two. You'll hear two white notes, followed by one black, at a faster clip than in previous sessions. At this point, you might find yourself getting impatient and wanting to charge ahead to the end of the book. But please do take your time, completing all of the drills even if you find them unnecessary.

Track 33	Track 34	Track 35
1.	1.	1.
2.	2.	2.
3.	3.	3.
4.	4.	4.
5.	5.	5.
6.	6.	6.
7.	7.	7.
8.	8.	8.
9.	9.	9.
10.	10.	10.
11.	11.	11.
12.	12.	12.

WEEK 5 — SESSION 31

Start this session by picking any black pitch you'd like to explore. Just as you've done in many of the other sessions, put the note under the microscope and listen to it over and over again, until new subtleties emerge. Then, as usual, clear your ears before moving on to the identification exercises.

We'll compare the white and black notes one more time with today's drill, on **Tracks 36–38** of **Audio 2**. The pattern this time is two black notes, followed by one white. Of course, limiting the possibilities like this is, in a way, making things easier for you to identify. But on the other hand, this does not preclude your really digging in to hear the individual flavors throughout the drills.

Track 36	Track 37	Track 38
1.	1.	1.
2.	2.	2.
3.	3.	3.
4.	4.	4.
5.	5.	5.
6.	6.	6.
7.	7.	7.
8.	8.	8.
9.	9.	9.
10.	10.	10.
11.	11.	11.
12.	12.	12.

WEEK 5 — SESSION 32

We'll now take a different approach and for the next few drills work with diminished seventh chords. In these harmonies, all the notes are spaced a minor third apart. Each note therefore has equal weight, so it will be difficult to find a single note to latch onto as a home base.

In this session we'll work only with the notes of a C diminished seventh chord, whose technically correct spelling is C–E♭–G♭–B♭♭. However, feel free to call the notes other names, for example A instead of B♭♭. (Astute readers will note that these same notes also form E♭, G♭, and A diminished seventh chords.)

Play the C diminished seventh chord on a keyboard or other instrument; arpeggiate the notes if your axe is a monophonic one. Study the chord as a whole and of course focus on the individual notes as well.

Now take a stab at identifying the notes on **Tracks 39–41** of **Audio 41**. You might find yourself slightly disoriented in these exercises—just take it easy and trust in your newfound abilities to decipher the individual flavors of the four notes. Feel free to pause the audio whenever needed.

Track 39	Track 40	Track 41
1.	1.	1.
2.	2.	2.
3.	3.	3.
4.	4.	4.
5.	5.	5.
6.	6.	6.
7.	7.	7.
8.	8.	8.
9.	9.	9.
10.	10.	10.
11.	11.	11.
12.	12.	12.
13.	13.	13.
14.	14.	14.
15.	15.	15.

WEEK 5 — SESSION 33

These next drills are similar to the last session's, but instead of C, they're based on a C♯ diminished seventh chord—that's C♯–E–G–B♭. To start today's work, compare the overall flavor of the C♯ diminished seventh chord to that of the C diminished seventh. Take some time to savor the individual notes within the former chord, too.

Once you're ready, try identifying the notes C♯, E, G, and B♭ in the drills on **Tracks 42–44** of **Audio 2**. How did this session go—was it any more difficult for you to identify the notes from the C♯ diminished seventh chord than from the C diminished seventh chord?

Track 42	Track 43	Track 44
1.	1.	1.
2.	2.	2.
3.	3.	3.
4.	4.	4.
5.	5.	5.
6.	6.	6.
7.	7.	7.
8.	8.	8.
9.	9.	9.
10.	10.	10.
11.	11.	11.
12.	12.	12.
13.	13.	13.
14.	14.	14.
15.	15.	15.

WEEK 5 — SESSION 34

The ante is upped in today's session, which involves eight notes—those from both the C and C# diminished seventh chords, C–E♭–G♭–B♭♭ (which you might hear as an A♮) and C#–E–G–B♭.

You'll be asked to choose from these eight pitches in identifying the drills on **Tracks 45–47** of **Audio 2**. This has the potential to be a dizzying exercise, so we'll slow things down a little bit on the audio, to give a chance to really hear the notes before identifying them. But this is just a temporary deceleration—things will get a bit faster in your next session.

Before you move on, be sure to assess your identification of this drill, and to spend a little extra time listening deeply to any notes that might be tripping you up.

Track 45	Track 46	Track 47
1.	1.	1.
2.	2.	2.
3.	3.	3.
4.	4.	4.
5.	5.	5.
6.	6.	6.
7.	7.	7.
8.	8.	8.
9.	9.	9.
10.	10.	10.
11.	11.	11.
12.	12.	12.
13.	13.	13.
14.	14.	14.
15.	15.	15.
16.	16.	16.
17.	17.	17.
18.	18.	18.
19.	19.	19.
20.	20.	20.

WEEK 5 – SESSION 35

Many of the drills so far have featured long tones, with ample time between notes for you to process and identify the sonorities. In actuality, notes often whiz by our ears like cars on the freeway, so now we'll do some work that takes this into account.

On **Tracks 48–50** of **Audio 2**, you'll find notes that are played staccato and go by a bit more quickly than in previous drills. The exercise won't be as formidable as it might sound, though, as you'll be dealing with only the seven white notes. When you do this work, don't stop the audio at any point; if you can't process a tone in time, just skip it and move on to the next one.

Track 48	Track 49	Track 50
1.	1.	1.
2.	2.	2.
3.	3.	3.
4.	4.	4.
5.	5.	5.
6.	6.	6.
7.	7.	7.
8.	8.	8.
9.	9.	9.
10.	10.	10.
11.	11.	11.
12.	12.	12.
13.	13.	13.
14.	14.	14.
15.	15.	15.
16.	16.	16.
17.	17.	17.
18.	18.	18.
19.	19.	19.
20.	20.	20.
21.	21.	21.
22.	22.	22.
23.	23.	23.
24.	24.	24.

WEEK 6 – SESSION 36

Let's not forget our sharps and flats, each with its distinctive flavor. If you'd like, before taking today's drill, play around with any of the black-key notes that you still don't feel completely confident in identifying.

Next play **Tracks 51–53** of **Audio 2**. Like yesterday's session, these have a relatively quick series of notes, with only black-key pitches, their durations cut short, for you to identify. Don't feel bad if any of the notes slip by you; this doesn't mean that you're aurally deficient. You might be intimately familiar with something, but if it goes by in a blur, it can be problematic to identify.

Track 51	Track 52	Track 53
1.	1.	1.
2.	2.	2.
3.	3.	3.
4.	4.	4.
5.	5.	5.
6.	6.	6.
7.	7.	7.
8.	8.	8.
9.	9.	9.
10.	10.	10.
11.	11.	11.
12.	12.	12.
13.	13.	13.
14.	14.	14.
15.	15.	15.
16.	16.	16.
17.	17.	17.
18.	18.	18.
19.	19.	19.
20.	20.	20.
21.	21.	21.
22.	22.	22.
23.	23.	23.
24.	24.	24.

WEEK 6 – SESSION 37

By now you've spent plenty of time getting to know each of the 12 pitches inside and out. With any luck, the subtleties inherent to each of the notes are becoming second-hand to you, and your ears have really opened up over the course of your perfect-pitch training.

You're probably ready for the speed drills on **Tracks 54–56** of **Audio 2**, which feature all 12 tones. Again, don't pause the audio if you can't name a note immediately. Take the whole test without stopping, and without thinking too much about the identities of the notes. Use snap judgments to identify these flavors and then check your work before moving on to the final sessions with piano-based notes.

Track 54	Track 55	Track 56
1.	1.	1.
2.	2.	2.
3.	3.	3.
4.	4.	4.
5.	5.	5.
6.	6.	6.
7.	7.	7.
8.	8.	8.
9.	9.	9.
10.	10.	10.
11.	11.	11.
12.	12.	12.
13.	13.	13.
14.	14.	14.
15.	15.	15.
16.	16.	16.
17.	17.	17.
18.	18.	18.
19.	19.	19.
20.	20.	20.
21.	21.	21.
22.	22.	22.
23.	23.	23.
24.	24.	24.

WEEK 6 — SESSION 38

We'll slow things back down a little now and do some harmonic work involving groupings of four notes—sonorities whose individual flavors, in some instances, might be a challenge to pull apart.

To help you out, the clusters you'll hear on **Tracks 1–3** of **Audio 3** include only the black-key notes. Each sonority is played twice, for a generous duration, and there is sufficient space between the examples for you to play the individual notes in your head and then identify them. Even so, feel free to pause the audio at any point, to better assess the tones in your ear.

Track 1	Track 2	Track 3
1.	1.	1.
2.	2.	2.
3.	3.	3.
4.	4.	4.
5.	5.	5.
6.	6.	6.
7.	7.	7.
8.	8.	8.
9.	9.	9.
10.	10.	10.

WEEK 6 — SESSION 39

We'll spend one more session with four-note groupings, this time focusing on the white-key notes—sounds that once again will stretch your ears as you extract the individual flavors.

Turn on **Tracks 4–6** of **Audio 3** to try today's drills. Remember not to strain, and to let the flavors inside each group of notes come to you, because it's harder to listen deeply—or do anything, for that matter—when one is tense. If the drills give you trouble, try playing some clusters of your own on the piano. This will make it easier to isolate the individual notes from these masses of sounds. These are among the most challenging drills in the sessions; don't beat yourself up if you have to spend a bit of extra time with the sounds.

Track 4	Track 5	Track 6
1.	1.	1.
2.	2.	2.
3.	3.	3.
4.	4.	4.
5.	5.	5.
6.	6.	6.
7.	7.	7.
8.	8.	8.
9.	9.	9.
10.	10.	10.

WEEK 6 — SESSION 40

Over the course of these sessions, you've learned to listen to pitches in all new ways. You've developed an awareness of pitch that you probably hadn't had before, even if you're a seasoned musician with decades of practice under your belt. Now try a final perfect-pitch test, using notes played on the piano, on **Tracks 7–8** of **Audio 3**. You'll likely be very satisfied by the progress you've made since you began this ear training.

Play **Track 7** and write a note name next to each number, choosing from the white-key notes:

1.	2.	3.	4.
5.	6.	7.	8.
9.	10.	11.	12.
13.	14.	15.	16.
17.	18.	19.	20.
21.	22.	23.	24.

Now try **Track 8** of **Audio 3** and write in the notes, including all 12 pitches, you hear:

1.	2.	3.	4.
5.	6.	7.	8.
9.	10.	11.	12.
13.	14.	15.	16.
17.	18.	19.	20.
21.	22.	23.	24.

WEEK 6 — SESSION 41

All the previous drills have been on the piano, so in the last exercises of this book we'll work with other instruments, starting with the violin, to get you started in a more universal direction. Listen deeply to **Track 9** of **Audio 3**, where you'll hear that instrument playing a C in long tones; the same note is played on both the violin and piano on **Track 10**, for timbral comparison.

Now try drill the drills on **Tracks 11–13**, which incorporate only the white-key notes as played on the violin. After you fill in your responses, do a little self-assessment. How did the exercise go? Is it harder for you to hear notes on the violin than the piano, or equivalent? If the latter (and you're not a violinist), that's great—you already have excellent universal hearing!

Track 11	Track 12	Track 13
1.	1.	1.
2.	2.	2.
3.	3.	3.
4.	4.	4.
5.	5.	5.
6.	6.	6.
7.	7.	7.
8.	8.	8.
9.	9.	9.
10.	10.	10.
11.	11.	11.
12.	12.	12.
13.	13.	13.
14.	14.	14.
15.	15.	15.

WEEK 6 – SESSION 42

Today let's focus on the black-key notes as played on the violin. On **Track 14** of **Audio 3**, you can luxuriate in the note F♯ played by a violinist. Try to look past the timbre and listen for the flavor's universal qualities before listening to the note played both on the violin and the piano on **Track 15**.

Test yourself on all five sharps/flats as played on the violin by listening to **Tracks 16–18**. Can you hear the tones more as pitch flavors and less as violin sounds? If not, repeat the exercise that you began with this session. And don't feel frustrated—it might take a bit of time for your ears to get past the timbral differences.

Track 16	Track 17	Track 18
1.	1.	1.
2.	2.	2.
3.	3.	3.
4.	4.	4.
5.	5.	5.
6.	6.	6.
7.	7.	7.
8.	8.	8.
9.	9.	9.
10.	10.	10.
11.	11.	11.
12.	12.	12.
13.	13.	13.
14.	14.	14.
15.	15.	15.

WEEK 7 – SESSION 43

We'll focus on the violin for one last session. Start by listening deeply to **Track 19** of **Audio 3**, featuring the note A. Again, listen for the note's A-ness and not the characteristic sound of the instrument, with the bow traveling over the string. Then, compare an A on the violin and the piano on **Track 20**.

After spending a bit of time with the A, try the drills on **Tracks 21–23**, which feature all 12 pitches in a pattern that goes like this: C, random tone; C random tone; etc. After you've completed the drills, if you feel deficient, you might have a violin-playing friend use his or her instrument to drill you on pitches.

Track 21	Track 22	Track 23
1.	1.	1.
2.	2.	2.
3.	3.	3.
4.	4.	4.
5.	5.	5.
6.	6.	6.
7.	7.	7.
8.	8.	8.
9.	9.	9.
10.	10.	10.
11.	11.	11.
12.	12.	12.
13.	13.	13.
14.	14.	14.
15.	15.	15.

WEEK 7 — SESSION 44

Let's switch to a woodwind instrument—the flute—for this next series of exercises. The flute of course features an entirely different timbre than the violin, as you can hear on **Track 24** of **Audio 3**, featuring the note C. After you've bathed in the flute's C, compare it to that of the piano by listening to **Track 25**.

The drills on **Tracks 26–28** focus on the white-key notes played on the flute. As always, delve deeply into each note as you identify its flavor. If you're not a woodwind player, did you experience any difficulties in doing these exercises? Why do you think that is, and how could you get past the timbre of the flute just to focus on the notes?

Track 26	Track 27	Track 28
1.	1.	1.
2.	2.	2.
3.	3.	3.
4.	4.	4.
5.	5.	5.
6.	6.	6.
7.	7.	7.
8.	8.	8.
9.	9.	9.
10.	10.	10.
11.	11.	11.
12.	12.	12.
13.	13.	13.
14.	14.	14.
15.	15.	15.

WEEK 7 — SESSION 45

Now we'll move to the black-key notes as rendered on the flute. Play **Track 29** of **Audio 3** to meditate on the note F♯, the same flavor that you're so familiar with on the piano. Then advance to **Track 30** to hear the same note played on both the flute and the piano.

When you're ready, test yourself with **Tracks 31–33**, featuring the F♯ and its four black-key cohorts. With any luck, your ears are starting to look past the timbral surfaces of the notes, to get deep inside the flavors. How does your hearing of these notes compare with the way you process pitches on the piano and violin?

Track 31	Track 32	Track 33
1.	1.	1.
2.	2.	2.
3.	3.	3.
4.	4.	4.
5.	5.	5.
6.	6.	6.
7.	7.	7.
8.	8.	8.
9.	9.	9.
10.	10.	10.
11.	11.	11.
12.	12.	12.
13.	13.	13.
14.	14.	14.
15.	15.	15.

WEEK 7 – SESSION 46

Let's spend one more session focusing on the flute. Begin by playing **Track 34** of **Audio 3**, to meditate on the note A. Ignore the clues of the instrument's identity, like the breathing, and let the sound of the pure pitch wash over your ears. Then, play **Track 35** to hear how the A sounds on the flute relative to how it sounds on the piano.

After spending a bit of time with the A, try the drills on **Tracks 36–38**, which feature all 12 pitches in a pattern that goes like this: C, random tone; C random tone; etc. After you've completed the drills, if you feel deficient, you might have a flute-playing friend use his or her instrument to drill you on pitches.

Track 36	Track 37	Track 38
1.	1.	1.
2.	2.	2.
3.	3.	3.
4.	4.	4.
5.	5.	5.
6.	6.	6.
7.	7.	7.
8.	8.	8.
9.	9.	9.
10.	10.	10.
11.	11.	11.
12.	12.	12.
13.	13.	13.
14.	14.	14.
15.	15.	15.

WEEK 7 — SESSION 47

In the last few sessions, we'll explore pitch on instruments that are at the core of a typical pop or rock group—the electric guitar and the electric bass. Because of the commonness of these instruments in so many different types of music, it's useful to do some ear training with them.

To hear how the middle C on a guitar (on the first fret of the second string) sounds compared to that on the piano, listen to **Track 39** of **Audio 3**. Then, try the drills on **Tracks 40–42**, which contain only white-key notes using both fretted and open strings. Do this exercise even if you're a guitarist and are already very familiar with the notes on the instrument.

Track 40	Track 41	Track 42
1.	1.	1.
2.	2.	2.
3.	3.	3.
4.	4.	4.
5.	5.	5.
6.	6.	6.
7.	7.	7.
8.	8.	8.
9.	9.	9.
10.	10.	10.
11.	11.	11.
12.	12.	12.

WEEK 7 — SESSION 48

We'll begin this session by listening to how a black-key note—specifically, the G string's third-fret B♭—sounds on the guitar. Listen carefully to **Track 43** of **Audio 3** to hear that note compared to the same pitch on the piano.

After a brief pause, try the drills on **Tracks 44–46**, which pit the open A string against random notes drawn from the 12 pitches. All the notes in these exercises have distortion—which, with its surplus of overtones, might make it tricky for some listeners to judge the pitches.

Track 44	Track 45	Track 46
1.	1.	1.
2.	2.	2.
3.	3.	3.
4.	4.	4.
5.	5.	5.
6.	6.	6.
7.	7.	7.
8.	8.	8.
9.	9.	9.
10.	10.	10.
11.	11.	11.
12.	12.	12.

WEEK 7 — SESSION 49

Let's close out these sessions by listening to a C played on the bass guitar, next to the same note played on the piano, as heard on **Track 47** of **Audio 3**. Note that the piano is playing middle C, and the bass is playing the C an octave below.

After you've scrutinized the timbral differences between the bass guitar and the piano, do the drills on **Tracks 48–50**, where you'll hear the bass playing an open A string, then another pitch. Write the name of the second pitch in the space provided.

Track 48	Track 49	Track 50
1.	1.	1.
2.	2.	2.
3.	3.	3.
4.	4.	4.
5.	5.	5.
6.	6.	6.
7.	7.	7.
8.	8.	8.
9.	9.	9.
10.	10.	10.
11.	11.	11.
12.	12.	12.

Now that you've completed these sessions, consider extending your perfect-pitch exercises to other instruments. If, for example, you've got a friend who's an alto saxophonist, have him or her drill you using notes on that instrument. (Make certain your friend knows you are answering in concert key, and not as played.)

Also, be sure to take stock of your progress during these sessions. If there are any lingering weak areas—for instance, maybe it's difficult for you to pull apart harmonic clusters of notes—spend extra time to correct these problems. Review these sessions at any time; if you run out of drills on the audio, you can always have a partner make up some drills, or you can even make your own exercises by inputting the notes and using the playback feature on a program like Finale or Sibelius.

Most important—and we can't stress this enough—always listen, listen, listen. And then listen some more!

ANSWER KEYS FOR SESSIONS

Session 4, Track 10

Session 5, Track 11

Session 5, Track 12

Session 6, Track 13

Session 6, Track 14

Session 7, Track 15

Session 8, Track 16

Session 8, Track 17

Session 9, Track 18

Session 9, Track 19

Session 9, Track 20

Session 10, Track 21

Session 10, Track 22

Session 10, Track 23

Session 11, Track 24

Session 15, Track 36

Session 15, Track 37

Session 16, Track 38

Session 16, Track 39

Session 16, Track 40

Session 17, Track 41

Session 17, Track 42

Session 17, Track 43

Session 18, Track 44

Session 18, Track 45

Session 18, Track 46

Session 19, Track 1

Session 19, Track 2

Session 19, Track 3

Session 20, Track 4

Session 20, Track 5

Session 20, Track 6

Session 21, Track 7

Session 21, Track 8

Session 21, Track 9

Session 22, Track 10

Session 22, Track 11

Session 22, Track 12

Session 23, Track 13

Session 23, Track 14

Session 24, Track 15

Session 24, Track 16

Session 24, Track 17

Session 25, Track 18

Session 25, Track 19

Session 25, Track 20

Session 26, Track 21

Session 26, Track 22

Session 26, Track 23

Session 27, Track 24

Session 27, Track 25

Session 27, Track 26

Session 28, Track 27

Session 28, Track 28

Session 28, Track 29

Session 29, Track 30

Session 29, Track 31

Session 29, Track 32

Session 30, Track 33

Session 30, Track 34

Session 30, Track 35

Session 31, Track 36

Session 31, Track 37

Session 31, Track 38

Session 32, Track 39

Session 32, Track 40

Session 32, Track 41

Session 33, Track 42

Session 33, Track 43

Session 33, Track 44

Session 34, Track 45

Session 34, Track 46

Session 34, Track 47

Session 35, Track 48

Session 35, Track 49

Session 35, Track 50

Session 36, Track 51

Session 36, Track 52

Session 36, Track 53

Session 37, Track 54

Session 37, Track 55

Session 37, Track 56

Session 38, Track 1

Session 38, Track 2

Session 38, Track 3

Session 39, Track 4

Session 39, Track 5

Session 39, Track 6

Session 40, Track 7

Session 40, Track 8

Session 41, Track 11

Session 41, Track 12

Session 41, Track 13

Session 42, Track 16

Session 42, Track 17

Session 42, Track 18

Session 43, Track 21

Session 43, Track 22

Session 43, Track 23

Session 44, Track 26

Session 44, Track 27

Session 44, Track 28

Session 45, Track 31

Session 45, Track 32

Session 45, Track 33

Session 46, Track 36

Session 46, Track 37

Session 46, Track 38

Session 47, Track 40
(Music sounds an octave lower than written.)

Session 47, Track 41
(Music sounds an octave lower than written.)

Session 47, Track 42
(Music sounds an octave lower than written.)

Session 48, Track 44
(Music sounds an octave lower than written.)

Session 48, Track 45
(Music sounds an octave lower than written.)

Session 48, Track 46
(Music sounds an octave lower than written.)

Session 49, Track 48

Session 49, Track 49

Session 49, Track 50

SUGGESTIONS FOR FURTHER READING

Bachem, A. "Various Types of Absolute Pitch," *JASA* ix (1937): 146–51.

Bachem, A. "Time Factors in Relative and Absolute Pitch Determination," *JASA* xxvi (1954): 751–3.

Baggaley, J. "Measurement of Absolute Pitch," *Psychology of Music* xxii/1 (1974): 11–17.

Burns, E.M. and S.L. Campbell. "Frequency and Frequency-Ratio Resolution by Possessors of Absolute and Relative Pitch: Examples of Categorical Perception?" *JASA* xcvi (1994): 2704–19.

Brady, P.T.: 'Fixed Scale Mechanism of Absolute Pitch', *JASA*, xlviii (1970), 883–7

Chaloupka, V., S. Mitchell and R. Muirhead. "Observation of a Reversible, Medication- Induced Change in Pitch Perception," *JASA* xcvi (1994): 145–9.

Clarkson, M.G. and R.K. Clifton. "Infant Pitch Perception: Evidence from Responding to Pitch Categories and the Missing Fundamental," *JASA* lxxvii (1985): 1521–8.

Costall, A. "The Relativity of Absolute Pitch," *Musical Structure and Cognition*, ed. P. Howell, I. Cross and R. West (London, 1985): 189–208.

Cuddy, L.L. "Practice Effects in the Absolute Judgment of Pitch," *JASA* xliii (1968): 1069–76.

Cuddy, L.L. "Training the Absolute Identification of Pitch," *Perception and Psychophysics* viii (1970): 265–9.

D'Amato, M.R. "A Search for Tonal Pattern Perception in Cebus Monkeys: Why Monkeys Can't Hum a Tune," *Music Perception* v (1987–8): 453–80.

Halpern, A.R. "Memory for the Absolute Pitch of Familiar Songs," *Memory and Cognition* xvii (1989): 572–81.

Heaton, C.P. "Air Ball: Spontaneous Large-Group Precision Chanting," *Popular Music and Society* xvi/1 (1992): 81–4.

Hulse, S.H., J. Cynx and J. Humpal. "Absolute and Relative Pitch Discrimination in Serial Pitch Perception by Birds," *Journal of Experimental Psychology: General* cxiii (1984): 38–54.

Jeffress, L.A. "Absolute Pitch," *JASA* xxxiv (1962): 987.

Lecanuet, J.-P. "L'expérience auditive prénatale," *Naissance et développement du sens musical*, ed. I. Deliège and J.A. Sloboda (Paris, 1995): 7–37; English translation as *Musical Beginnings* (Oxford, 1996): 3–34.

Levitin, D.J. "Absolute Memory for Musical Pitch: Evidence from the Production of Learned Melodies," *Perception & Psychophysics* lvi (1994): 414–23.

Levitin, D.J. "Absolute Pitch: Self-Reference and Human Memory," International *Journal of Computing Anticipatory Systems* iv (1999): 255–266.

Lockhead, G.R. and R. Byrd. "Practically Perfect Pitch," *JASA* lxx (1981): 387–9.

Meyer, M. "Is the Memory of Absolute Pitch Capable of Development by Training?" *Psychological Review* vi (1899), 514–16.

Miyazaki, K. "Musical Pitch Identification by Absolute Pitch Possessors," *Perception & Psychophysics* xliv (1988): 501–12.

Miyazaki, K. Absolute Pitch Identification: Effects of Timbre and Pitch Region," *Music Perception* vii (1989–90): 1–14.

Miyazaki, K. "Perception of Musical Intervals by Absolute Pitch Possessors," *Music Perception* ix (1991–2): 413–26.

Miyazaki, K. "Absolute Pitch as an Inability: Identification of Musical Intervals in a Tonal Context," *Music Perception* xi (1993–4): 55–71.

Moore, B.C.J. *An Introduction to the Psychology of Hearing.* San Diego: Academic Press, 1997.

Peacock, K. "Synaesthetic Perception: Alexander Skriabin's Colour Hearing," *Music Perception* ii (1984–5): 483–506.

Profita, J.and T.G. Bidder. "Perfect Pitch," *American Journal of Medical Genetics* xxix (1988): 763–71.

Rakowski, A. and M. Morawska-Büngeler. "In Search of the Criteria for Absolute Pitch," *Archives of Acoustics* xii (1987): 198–207.

Révész, G. *Zur Grundlegung der Tonpsychologie*. Leipzig: Veit, 1913.

Rogers, G.L. "Four Cases of Pitch-Specific Chromesthesia in Trained Musicians with Absolute Pitch," *Psychology of Music* xv/1 (1987): 198–207.

Rosch, E. "Cognitive Representations of Semantic Categories," *Journal of Experimental Psychology: General* civ (1975): 192–223.

Schlaug, G. et al. "In Vivo Evidence of Structural Brain Asymmetry in Musicians," *Science* cclxvii (1995): 699–701.

Sergeant, D.: "Experimental Investigation of Absolute Pitch," *JRME* xvii (1969): 135–43.

Sergeant, D.C. and S. Roche. "Perceptual Shifts in the Auditory Information Processing of Young Children, "*Psychology of Music* i/1 (1973): 39–48.

Siegel, J.A. "Sensory and Verbal Coding Strategies in Subjects with Absolute Pitch," *Journal of Experimental Psychology* ciii (1974): 37–44.

Slonimsky, N. *Perfect Pitch: a Life Story.* Oxford: Oxford University Press, 1988.

Stevens, S.S. "The Relation of Pitch to Intensity," *JASA* vii (1935): 150–54.

Takeuchi, A.H. and S.H. Hulse. "Absolute-Pitch Judgments of Black- and White-Key Pitches," *Music Perception* ix (1991–2): 27–46.

Terhardt, E. and M. Seewan. "Aural Key Identification and Its Relationship to Absolute Pitch," *Music Perception* i (1983–4): 63–83.

Tooze, Z.J., F.H. Harrington and J.C. Fentress. "Individually Distinct Vocalizations in Timber Wolves 'canis lupus,'" *Animal Behavior* xl (1990): 723–30.

Vernon, E. "Absolute Pitch: a Case Study," *British Journal of Psychology* lxviii (1977): 485–9.

Ward, W.D. "Absolute Pitch," *The Psychology of Music*, ed. D. Deutsch (New York: Academic Press, 1982, 2/1999): 265–98.

Watt, H.J. *The Psychology of Sound*. Cambridge: University Press, 1917.

Wedell, C.H. "The Nature of Absolute Judgment of Pitch," *Journal of Experimental Psychology* xvii (1934): 485–503.

Wellek, A. Das absolute Gehör und seine Typen," *Beihefte zur Zeitschrift für Angewandte Psychologie und Charakterkunde* lxxxiii (1938): 1–368.

Wynn, V.T. "Absolute Pitch Revisited," *British Journal of Psychology* lxxxiii (1992): 129–31.

Zatorre, R.J. and C. Beckett. "Multiple Coding Strategies in the Retention of Musical Tones by Possessors of Absolute Pitch," *Memory and Cognition* xvii (1989): 582–89.

ABOUT THE AUTHOR

Adam Perlmutter is a freelance writer, transcriber, and engraver living in Los Angeles, California. He contributes to *Premier Guitar*, *Acoustic Guitar*, *Guitar Aficionado*, and other music magazines. As a senior editor of *Guitar One* magazine and music editor of *Guitar World Acoustic*, Adam transcribed and arranged hundreds of songs, wrote numerous instructional pieces and gear reviews, and interviewed such leading guitarists as Jim Hall, Al Di Meola, and John Pizzarelli. He has written a number of instructional books, including *Color Your Chords* and *Jim Hall: Signature Licks*.

Train Your Ears

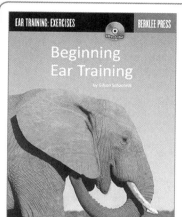

BEGINNING EAR TRAINING
by Gilson Schachnik
Berklee Press
Introduces the core skills of ear training. Teaches how to: learn melodies by ear; sight-sing; internalize rhythms and melodies; improve pitch and timing; transpose; use solfege; transcribe and notate; and much more!
50449548 Book/CD Pack $16.99

ESSENTIAL EAR TRAINING FOR THE CONTEMPORARY MUSICIAN
by Steve Prosser
Berklee Press
The Ear Training curriculum of Berklee College of Music is known and respected throughout the world. Now, for the first time, this unique method has been captured in one comprehensive book by the chair of the Ear Training Department. This method teaches musicians to hear the music they are seeing, notate the music they have composed or arranged, develop their music vocabulary, and understand the music they are hearing. The book features a complete course with text and musical examples, and studies in rhythm, sight recognition, sol-fa, and melody.
50449421 .... $16.95

BERKLEE MUSIC THEORY – 2ND EDITION
by Paul Schmeling
Book/CD Packs
Berklee Press
This essential method features rigorous, hands-on, "ears-on" practice exercises that help you explore the inner working of music, presenting notes, scales, and rhythms as they are heard in pop, jazz, and blues. You will learn and build upon the basic concepts of music theory with written exercises, listening examples, and ear training exercises. The included CD will help reinforce lessons as you begin to build a solid musical foundation. Now available with an answer key!
50449615 Book 1 .... $24.99
50449616 Book 2 .... $22.99

MUSIC THEORY WORKBOOK
For All Musicians
by Chris Bowman
A self-study course with illustrations & examples for you to write & check your answers. Topics include: major and minor scales; modes and other scales; harmony; intervals; chord structure; chord progressions and substitutions; and more. This workbook contains essential "backbone" concepts for working musicians. These are the things you must know. It may take a year to work through and thoroughly understand and memorize all that is in this book – and a lifetime to perfect it. But that's okay: You will own this valuable resource and have it for handy reference.
00101379 .... $12.99

ULTIMATE EAR TRAINING FOR GUITAR AND BASS
by Gary Willis
Everything you need to improve your ear training, including a CD with 99 full-demo tracks, vital information on intervals, rhythms, melodic shapes, inversions, scales, chords, extensions, alterations, fretboard visualization, and fingering diagrams.
00695182 Book/CD Pack $17.99

MUSIC THEORY
A Practical Guide for All Musicians
by Barrett Tagliarino
Get the rock-solid fundamentals of rhythm, pitch and harmony with this easy-to-use book/CD pack. Learn the universal language used by all musicians, regardless of instrument. Includes concise, detailed explanations, illustrations and written exercises with a full CD of examples and practice drills. This book will teach you how to: construct scales, chords and intervals • identify major and minor key centers and common chord progressions • accurately play various rhythm feels and figures • learn the basic principles of form and compositional analysis.
00311270 Book/CD Pack $14.95

HAL•LEONARD® CORPORATION
7777 W. Bluemound Rd. P.O. Box 13819 Milwaukee, WI 53213

www.halleonard.com

Prices, contents, and availability subject to change without notice.

Great Harmony & Theory Helpers

HAL LEONARD HARMONY & THEORY – PART 1: DIATONIC

by George Heussenstamm

This book is designed for anyone wishing to expand their knowledge of music theory, whether beginner or more advanced. The first two chapters deal with music fundamentals, and may be skipped by those with music reading experience. Each chapter contains many examples that clearly illustrate the concepts presented. Written exercises at the end of each chapter allow the reader to test and apply their knowledge. Topics include: basic music-reading instruction; triads in root position; triads in inversion; cadences; non-harmonic tones; the dominant seventh chord; other seventh chords; and more.

00312062.................................. $27.50

HAL LEONARD HARMONY & THEORY – PART 2: CHROMATIC

by George Heussenstamm

This two-book series includes a wealth of material used to teach harmony and theory in college-level courses by George Heussenstamm, author of the *Norton Manual of Musical Notation*. *Part 2 – Chromatic* introduces readers to modulation and more advanced harmonies, covering: secondary dominants; borrowed chords; the Neapolitan 6th chord; augmented 6th chords; 9th, 11th and 13th chords; and more. In addition to text, the book features many musical examples that illustrate the concepts, and exercises that allow readers to test and apply their knowledge.

00312064.................................. $27.50

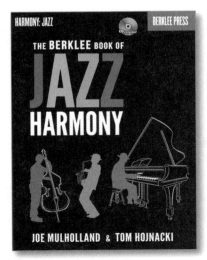

THE BERKLEE BOOK OF JAZZ HARMONY

by Joe Mulholland & Tom Hojnacki
Berklee Press

Learn jazz harmony, as taught at Berklee College of Music. This text provides a strong foundation in harmonic principles, supporting further study in jazz composition, arranging, and improvisation. It covers basic chord types and their tensions, with practical demonstrations of how they are used in characteristic jazz contexts and an accompanying recording that lets you hear how they can be applied.

00113755 Book/CD Pack $24.99

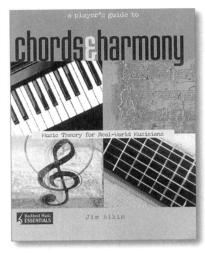

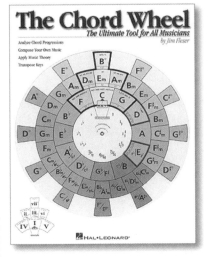

A PLAYER'S GUIDE TO CHORDS AND HARMONY

Music Theory for Real-World Musicians

by Jim Aikin
Backbeat Books

If you'd like to know about music theory but don't want to get bogged down in a stuffy college-level textbook, this guide was written just for you! It's a practical, no-nonsense book ideal for: young musicians learning guitar so they can play rock, folk or blues; DJs who've started recording their own tracks and need to know how chord progressions work; anyone who wants to play from the chord symbols in sheet music; classical musicians who want to do more than just "read the dots," and countless others. Covers: intervals, scales, modes, triads and advanced voicings; interpreting chord symbols and reading sheet music; voice leading, chord progressions and basic song forms; classical, jazz & pop; and more, with helpful quizzes and answers.

00331173.................................. $19.95

ENCYCLOPEDIA OF READING RHYTHMS

Text and Workbook for All Instruments

by Gary Hess
Musicians Institute Press

A comprehensive guide to: notes, rests, counting, subdividing, time signatures, triplets, ties, dotted notes and rests, cut time, compound time, swing, shuffle, rhythm studies, counting systems, road maps and more!

00695145 .... $19.95

THE CHORD WHEEL

The Ultimate Tool for All Musicians

by Jim Fleser

Master chord theory ... in minutes! *The Chord Wheel* is a revolutionary device that puts the most essential and practical applications of chord theory into your hands. This tool will help you: Improvise and Solo – Talk about chops! Comprehend key structure like never before; Transpose Keys – Instantly transpose any progression into each and every key; Compose Your Own Music – Watch your songwriting blossom! No music reading is necessary.

00695579 .... $14.99

HAL•LEONARD® CORPORATION

7777 W. BLUEMOUND RD. P.O. BOX 13819 MILWAUKEE, WI 53213

www.halleonard.com

Jazz Instruction & Improvisation

BOOKS FOR ALL INSTRUMENTS FROM HAL LEONARD

AN APPROACH TO JAZZ IMPROVISATION
by Dave Pozzi
Musicians Institute Press
Explore the styles of Charlie Parker, Sonny Rollins, Bud Powell and others with this comprehensive guide to jazz improvisation. Covers: scale choices • chord analysis • phrasing • melodies • harmonic progressions • more.
00695135 Book/CD Pack......................$17.95

THE ART OF MODULATING
FOR PIANISTS AND JAZZ MUSICIANS
by Carlos Salzedo &
Lucile Lawrence
Schirmer
The Art of Modulating is a treatise originally intended for the harp, but this edition has been edited for use by intermediate keyboardists and other musicians who have an understanding of basic music theory. In its pages you will find: table of intervals; modulation rules; modulation formulas; examples of modulation; extensions and cadences; ten fragments of dances; five characteristic pieces; and more.
50490581 ....$19.99

BUILDING A JAZZ VOCABULARY
By Mike Steinel
A valuable resource for learning the basics of jazz from Mike Steinel of the University of North Texas. It covers: the basics of jazz • how to build effective solos • a comprehensive practice routine • and a jazz vocabulary of the masters.
00849911 ....$19.95

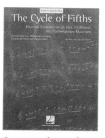

THE CYCLE OF FIFTHS
by Emile and Laura De Cosmo
This essential instruction book provides more than 450 exercises, including hundreds of melodic and rhythmic ideas. The book is designed to help improvisors master the cycle of fifths, one of the primary progressions in music. Guaranteed to refine technique, enhance improvisational fluency, and improve sight-reading!
00311114 ....$16.99

THE DIATONIC CYCLE
by Emile and Laura De Cosmo
Renowned jazz educators Emile and Laura De Cosmo provide more than 300 exercises to help improvisors tackle one of music's most common progressions: the diatonic cycle. This book is guaranteed to refine technique, enhance improvisational fluency, and improve sight-reading!
00311115 ....$16.95

EAR TRAINING
by Keith Wyatt,
Carl Schroeder and Joe Elliott
Musicians Institute Press
Covers: basic pitch matching • singing major and minor scales • identifying intervals • transcribing melodies and rhythm • identifying chords and progressions • seventh chords and the blues • modal interchange, chromaticism, modulation • and more.
00695198 Book/2-CD Pack...................$24.95

EXERCISES AND ETUDES FOR THE JAZZ INSTRUMENTALIST
by J.J. Johnson
Designed as study material and playable by any instrument, these pieces run the gamut of the jazz experience, featuring common and uncommon time signatures and keys, and styles from ballads to funk. They are progressively graded so that both beginners and professionals will be challenged by the demands of this wonderful music.
00842018 Bass Clef Edition $16.95
00842042 Treble Clef Edition $16.95

JAZZOLOGY
THE ENCYCLOPEDIA OF JAZZ THEORY FOR ALL MUSICIANS
by Robert Rawlins and
Nor Eddine Bahha
This comprehensive resource covers a variety of jazz topics, for beginners and pros of any instrument. The book serves as an encyclopedia for reference, a thorough methodology for the student, and a workbook for the classroom.
00311167 ....$19.99

JAZZ THEORY RESOURCES
by Bert Ligon
Houston Publishing, Inc.
This is a jazz theory text in two volumes. **Volume 1 includes**: review of basic theory • rhythm in jazz performance • triadic generalization • diatonic harmonic progressions and analysis • substitutions and turnarounds • and more. **Volume 2 includes**: modes and modal frameworks • quartal harmony • extended tertian structures and triadic superimposition • pentatonic applications • coloring "outside" the lines and beyond • and more.
00030458 Volume 1 ....$39.95
00030459 Volume 2 ....$29.95

JOY OF IMPROV
by Dave Frank
and John Amaral
This book/CD course on improvisation for all instruments and all styles will help players develop monster musical skills! Book One imparts a solid basis in technique, rhythm, chord theory, ear training and improv concepts. **Book Two** explores more advanced chord voicings, chord arranging techniques and more challenging blues and melodic lines. The CD can be used as a listening and play-along tool.
00220005 Book 1 – Book/CD Pack......................$27.99
00220006 Book 2 – Book/CD Pack......................$26.99

THE PATH TO JAZZ IMPROVISATION
by Emile and Laura De Cosmo
This fascinating jazz instruction book offers an innovative, scholarly approach to the art of improvisation. It includes in-depth analysis and lessons about: cycle of fifths • diatonic cycle • overtone series • pentatonic scale • harmonic and melodic minor scale • polytonal order of keys • blues and bebop scales • modes • and more.
00310904 ....$14.99

THE SOURCE
THE DICTIONARY OF CONTEMPORARY AND TRADITIONAL SCALES
by Steve Barta
This book serves as an informative guide for people who are looking for good, solid information regarding scales, chords, and how they work together. It provides right and left hand fingerings for scales, chords, and complete inversions. Includes over 20 different scales, each written in all 12 keys.
00240885 ....$18.99

21 BEBOP EXERCISES
by Steve Rawlins
This book/CD pack is both a warm-up collection and a manual for bebop phrasing. Its tasty and sophisticated exercises will help you develop your proficiency with jazz interpretation. It concentrates on practice in all twelve keys – moving higher by half-step – to help develop dexterity and range. The companion CD includes all of the exercises in 12 keys.
00315341 Book/CD Pack....................$17.95

HAL•LEONARD® CORPORATION
7777 W. BLUEMOUND RD. P.O. BOX 13819 MILWAUKEE, WI 53213

Visit Hal Leonard online at
www.halleonard.com

Prices, contents & availability
subject to change without notice.